CH

ZENDAYA
STAR PERFORMER

BY PEGGY CARAVANTES

Published by The Child's World®
1980 Lookout Drive • Mankato, MN 56003-1705
800-599-READ • www.childsworld.com

Photographs ©: Buckner/Variety/Rex Features/AP Images, cover, 1; Featureflash Photo Agency/Shutterstock Images, 5; WITT/SIPA/AP Images, 6; Kennell Krista/SIPA/AP Images, 8; Chris Pizzello/Invision/AP Images, 10; Peter Kramer/AP Images, 12; Charles Sykes/Invision/AP Images, 14, 16; Richard Shotwell/Invision/AP Images, 18; Matt Sayles/Invision/AP Images, 20

ISBN 9781503820005
LCCN 2016960924

Printed in the United States of America
PA02335

ABOUT THE AUTHOR

Peggy Caravantes is the author of over 25 nonfiction books for children and young adults. A retired educator, she enjoys research on almost any topic. Caravantes lives and writes in San Antonio, Texas, a city filled with history.

TABLE OF
CONTENTS

FAST FACTS

Name

- Zendaya Maree Stoermer Coleman

Birthdate

- September 1, 1996

Birthplace

- Oakland, California

Fun Trivia

- Zendaya means "to give thanks" in the Shona language of Zimbabwe.
- Zendaya's friends call her "Daya."
- Zendaya's **motto** is "don't forget to smile."[1]
- Burritos are Zendaya's favorite food, and her favorite dessert is coffee-flavored ice cream.

Chapter 1

EARLY YEARS

The day started with 14-year-old Zendaya sitting in her closet. It was late 2010, and she was trying to decide what to wear for her **audition**. She often spent hours trying to choose an outfit. She had been told she needed to wear more colors. But she liked black, white, and **neutral** colors best, except on her shoes. So she started by choosing her shoes. This time they were bright pink sneakers. With them, she wore black tights and a black decorated T-shirt.

By this time, Zendaya had lost count of how many auditions she had attended on her journey to become an actress, singer, and dancer. Despite the many rejections, Zendaya believed her dreams would someday be a reality. Her persistence paid off.

◀ **Zendaya and her costar, Bella Thorne, starred on the Disney Channel show *Shake It Up*.**

▲ In 2011, Zendaya went to the movie premiere of *Gnomeo & Juliet*.

Zendaya headed to Walt Disney Studios in Los Angeles, California. She was confident and ready to try out for the new television series *Shake It Up*. To get ready for the audition, she memorized all the lines for the character CeCe Jones.

The producer surprised her when she got to the studio. He asked her to read the part of Raquel "Rocky" Blue. Rocky, like CeCe, was a dancer and singer in the show. After reading opposite several girls playing CeCe, Zendaya got the part of Rocky. She wanted to pinch herself to be sure it was true.

> "Sometimes you can reach your destination by taking a totally different road."[3]
> —Zendaya

Zendaya's childhood had prepared her well for show business. Her mother managed the California Shakespeare Theater. She helped her mother seat people and sell tickets to support the theater.

Sometimes Zendaya got small parts in productions, such as *Twelfth Night* and *As You Like It*. Even as a little girl, she had big dreams. "I knew I wanted to be an entertainer," she said later. "I could see myself singing and dancing in front of millions of people."[2]

Chapter 2

RISING STAR

At six years old, Zendaya watched Raven-Symoné, lead singer for a popular teen group called the Cheetah Girls. As she listened to their music, she sang along with them. Zendaya told herself she could be like Raven. So she formed her own singing group.

A couple years later, she joined an Oakland, California, dance group called Future Shock. Zendaya danced hip-hop with them for several years. The first step she learned was how to freeze, or lock, to make a sudden pause in the dance. Then she threw herself into freestyle, stomping her bare feet and twirling around. She added to her hip-hop dancing ability by studying **hula** at the Academy of Hawaiian Arts.

◄ **Singing and dancing are two of Zendaya's passions.**

▲ **Zendaya and Bella became good friends during their time on the television show *Shake It Up*.**

Despite her dance performances, she was shy in elementary school. She never raised her hand in class and hated giving speeches in front of people.

But Zendaya had lost her shyness by the time she got her *Shake It Up* role.

In 2010, Zendaya made her television **debut**. Her costar was Bella Thorne, playing CeCe Jones. In the series, Rocky and CeCe are best friends who dream of becoming dancers. They succeed when they try out for *Shake It Up, Chicago*, and get parts as backup dancers.

Zendaya acted in the series until Disney canceled it in 2013. When asked what she would miss most, she said, "The cast, the crew, and every single person involved in our show were absolutely the greatest. . . . I will miss the fun we had every day on our set."[4]

"The secret to a really great friendship is just creating fun memories whenever you're with that person."[5]

—*Zendaya, on her friendship with Bella Thorne*

Chapter 3

SUPERSTAR

Zendaya was determined to do well. She joined *Dancing with the Stars* in 2013. She was the youngest dancer the show had ever had. Dancing in heels was tricky. She hung on to her partner to keep from falling. After a few days of dips, twirls, and backflips, every muscle in her body hurt. Ballroom dancing was difficult despite all her dance training. There were more rules, and posture and **elegance** were important. The routines were hard. She had to hold her head and hands in certain ways for each dance. But no one could tell that it was tough. She always flashed a big smile, even when she made mistakes. In an interview, she confessed: "I'm used to hip-hop dancing. . . . So I kind of have to forget what I know and restart all over again."[6]

◀ **Zendaya won second place on** ***Dancing with the Stars.***

▲ **Zendaya partnered with dancer Valentin Chmerkovskiy on *Dancing with the Stars*.**

Still, Zendaya practiced hard to learn the new dance styles. On the first night of the competition, she glided onto the stage, her purple and yellow skirt twirling. Cheers filled the auditorium. Her partner lifted her in the air, and she landed on her feet. Zendaya's steps matched her partner's exactly. That night, the pair topped the leader board. She performed a different dance style each week and finished in second place.

When asked if she would compete again, Zendaya said, "*Dancing with the Stars* was the most stressful thing I have ever done so I would say 'no' right now, but you know how people say, 'Never say never!'"[7]

After *Dancing with the Stars*, Zendaya began her own musical career. She released her first **single**, "Replay," in July of 2013. The song's music video featured plenty of dancing. But instead of the high heels and shiny dance floor, Zendaya wore high-top sneakers as she danced in an empty building. Her first album, *Zendaya*, followed later that year.

Also in 2013, she published an advice book. It was called: *Between U and Me: How to Rock Your Tween Years with Style and Confidence*. Zendaya mixed encouraging advice for her fans with hints about clothes, makeup, and friendship. "Just believe in yourself, in your ideas, in your dreams," she said. "You don't have to dance to anyone else's beat except your own."[8]

Disney Studios wanted their popular star back. But Zendaya had a requirement before she accepted any more Disney roles. She wanted more control over her parts. "The only way I was going to come back to the Disney Channel was if I was in a position of more power," she said.[9] Zendaya became the coproducer of Disney's *K. C. Undercover* as well as its lead actress. She plays K. C. Cooper, a teenage spy. In 2016, she received a Nickelodeon Kids' Choice Award for Favorite Female TV Star for that role. In accepting the award, she encouraged her young audience not to care what others think about them.

> "I have a really strong passion for what I do. I don't see myself doing anything else."[10]
>
> —*Zendaya, on her show business career*

◄ **When she was a teenager, Zendaya became a vegetarian. Her love for animals brought her to an animal rescue fundraiser in 2016.**

▲ Zendaya thanked her fans as she accepted her 2016 Kids' Choice Award.

With roles in two 2017 movies, *Spider-Man: Homecoming* and *The Greatest Showman on Earth*, Zendaya's career looks bright. She is also moving on to new projects. She created a line of shoes called Daya and plans to design a full line of clothing.

Zendaya believes that young people have an opportunity to change the world. She raises money for Convoy of Hope, a program to help feed women living in poverty. Whenever she speaks to her young fans, she encourages them to join her in raising their voices to help others.

THINK ABOUT IT

- Zendaya says that her motto is, "Don't forget to smile." What is another motto she seems to live by?
- In her book *Between U and Me*, Zendaya told her young readers, "Just believe in yourself, in your ideas, in your dreams."[11] Find at least two examples of Zendaya following her own advice.
- Zendaya encourages her fans to raise their voices to help others. Write a letter to Zendaya telling her how you help others in your school or community.

GLOSSARY

audition (aw-DISH-uhn): An audition is a short performance to test the talents of a musician, singer, dancer, or actor. Sometimes, Zendaya and Bella Thorne would audition for the same part.

debut (day-BYOO): A debut is a first public appearance or performance. Zendaya made her debut as an actress in the TV show *Shake It Up*.

elegance (EL-uh-guhns): Elegance is the quality of being graceful in style or movement. Zendaya learned to move with elegance during her time on *Dancing with the Stars*.

hula (HOO-lah): Hula is a dance that includes slow, rhythmic body movements. Taking hula lessons made Zendaya's body more flexible.

motto (MAH-toh): A motto is a short sentence that states someone's beliefs or is used as a rule for behavior. Zendaya's motto is "don't forget to smile."

neutral (NOO-truhl): Neutral colors are those that are pale and not bright, such as beige and gray. Zendaya prefers neutral colors, especially black and white.

producer (pruh-DOOS-ur): A producer is the person in charge of putting on a play or making a movie or TV program. Zendaya waited to see if the producer would give her a part in *Shake It Up*.

show business (SHOH BIZ-nis): Show business is popular entertainment, such as music, TV, and movies, and the industry that provides it. Zendaya quickly became a show business favorite with tweens and teens.

single (SING-guhl): A single is a recording that features one main song. Zendaya's first single sold over one million copies.

SOURCE NOTES

1. Zendaya. *Between U and Me: How to Rock Your Tween Years with Style and Confidence.* New York, NY: Disney Hyperion Books, 2013. Print. 4.

2. Ibid., 179.

3. Ibid., 184.

4. Elizabeth Wagmeister. "Last Dance: Bella Thorne and Zendaya Say Goodbye to *Shake It Up.*" *TV Guide.* CBS Interactive Inc., 7 Nov. 2013. Web. 20 Jan. 2017.

5. Lillian Chen. "Worth Noting: Zendaya Coleman." *Seventeen.com.* Hearst Communications Inc., 21 Aug. 2012. Web. 20 Jan. 2017.

6. "Zendaya Coleman—Reality Television Star, Singer, Television Actress." *Biography.* A&E Television Networks, Web. 20 Jan. 2017.

7. Elizabeth Wagmeister. "Last Dance: Bella Thorne and Zendaya Say Goodbye to *Shake It Up.*" *TV Guide.* CBS Interactive Inc., 7 Nov. 2013. Web. 20 Jan. 2017.

8. Zendaya. *Between U and Me: How to Rock Your Tween Years with Style and Confidence.* New York, NY: Disney Hyperion Books, 2013. Print. 4.

9. Hannah Orenstein. "The Real Reason Zendaya Has Stayed with Disney." *Seventeen.com.* Hearst Communications Inc., 2 Jun. 2016. Web. 20 Jan. 2017.

10. "6 of Our Favorite Quotes From Our Zendaya Interview." *jonesmagazine.com.* Jones Digital Inc., 1 Aug. 2013. Web. 20 Jan. 2017.

11. Zendaya. *Between U and Me: How to Rock Your Tween Years with Style and Confidence.* New York, NY: Disney Hyperion Books, 2013. Print. 8.

TO LEARN MORE

Books

Giovanni, Nikki. *Hip Hop Speaks to Children: A Celebration of Poetry with a Beat*. Naperville, IL: Sourcebooks Jabberwocky, 2008.

Schwartz, Heather E. *Zendaya: Capturing the Stage, Screen, and Modeling Scene*. Minneapolis, MN: Lerner, 2015.

Zendaya. *Between U and Me: How to Rock Your Tween Years with Style and Confidence*. New York, NY: Disney Hyperion Books, 2013.

Web Sites

Visit our Web site for links about Zendaya:

childsworld.com/links

Note to Parents, Teachers, and Librarians: We routinely verify our Web links to make sure they are safe and active sites. So encourage your readers to check them out!

INDEX